THE JESUS WAY

—SMALL BOOKS *of* RADICAL FAITH—

I0143209

Who Are Our Enemies

and How Do We Love Them?

HYUNG JIN KIM SUN

HERALD
PRESS

Harrisonburg, Virginia

Herald Press
PO Box 866, Harrisonburg, Virginia 22803
www.HeraldPress.com

Library of Congress Cataloging-in-Publication Data
Names: Kim Sun, Hyung Jin, author.
Title: Who are our enemies and how do we love them? / Hyung Jin Kim Sun.
Description: Harrisonburg, Virginia : Herald Press, 2020. | Series: The
  Jesus way: small books of radical faith | Includes bibliographical
  references.
Identifiers: LCCN 2020018812 (print) | LCCN 2020018813 (ebook) | ISBN
  9781513805696 (paperback) | ISBN 9781513806181 (ebook)
Subjects: LCSH: Love--Religious aspects--Christianity. | Enemies. |
  Nonviolence--Religious aspects--Christianity.
Classification: LCC BV4639 .K485 2020 (print) | LCC BV4639 (ebook) | DDC
  241/.4--dc23
LC record available at https://lccn.loc.gov/2020018812
LC ebook record available at https://lccn.loc.gov/2020018813

Study guides are available for many Herald Press titles at www.HeraldPress.com.

Unless otherwise noted, Scripture text is quoted, with permission, from the
New Revised Standard Version, © 1989, Division of Christian Education of the
National Council of Churches of Christ in the United States of America.

24 23 22 21 20   10 9 8 7 6 5 4 3 2 1

To my daughter, Loa Kim, who will soon walk into this beautiful but still violent world, and to all those who are witnessing the gospel of peace in every corner of this earth

Who Are Our Enemies

and How Do We Love Them?

"We are to love our enemies *because God loves them*. Hyung Jin Kim Sun takes Jesus' central teaching—neighbor love is God's love—at his word. As a teacher of peace with Asian roots and a third-world childhood, Kim Sun knows something about loving those who oppose us. He lives this love, and sees how the way to God leads not away from but toward and through care for the 'other,' no matter how 'other.' This book is good for the soul."

—**DAVID W. AUGSBURGER**, professor emeritus of pastoral care and counseling at Fuller Theological Seminary and author of *Caring Enough to Confront*

"How do Christians live faithfully in a violent world, contributing fruitful possibilities for peace? To answer, this book offers a very readable and helpful account of biblical, theological, and historical perspectives related to Christian peace practices. It is an excellent resource, inviting readers to consider what it means to live a Christian ethic of love amidst enemies and providing useful tools for deepening the witness of nonviolence. I highly recommend this book!"

—**THOMAS REYNOLDS**, associate professor of theology at Emmanuel College of Victoria University in the University of Toronto and author of *Vulnerable Communion: A Theology of Disability and Hospitality*

"Hyung Jin Kim Sun's eloquent testimony to the spirit and practice of Christian pacifism is incisive, clear, and persuasive. What takes this work far beyond 'classic' pacifism is Kim Sun's use of social sciences and history to make a strong case for the practical, political effectiveness of nonviolence. This move brings together all just war thinkers and pacifists committed to ending violence, whether direct and structural."

—**LISA SOWLE CAHILL**, J. Donald Monan Professor of Theology at Boston College and author of *Global Justice, Christology, and Christian Ethics*

"In clear, simple, and gentle language, Hyung Jin Kim Sun invites readers to a fresh conversation on the gospel of peace. A great deal of wisdom is packed into this short book as it moves from the biblical and historical dimensions of Christian pacifism to personal and structural applications. A perfect text for small groups or classroom use."

—**JOHN D. ROTH**, professor of history at Goshen College and author of *Choosing Against War*

"The Anabaptist tradition, and in particular the Mennonites, has long been a special gift to Canadian churches in exemplifying what it means to be citizens, peacebuilders, and active nonviolent changemakers. Hyung Jin Kim Sun furthers this deep, honorable, and Christlike legacy through his theologically informed yet practically oriented writing. This is an immediate, compelling, and accessible read for all who seek to live out their faith in all areas of life."

—**PETER NOTEBOOM**, general secretary of the Canadian Council of Churches

"Hyung Jin Kim Sun has written a very readable book that engages frequently asked questions about Anabaptist pacifism. It introduces biblical foundations as well as pragmatic considerations of nonviolence for readers new to the topic."

—**REINA NEUFELDT**, associate professor of peace and conflict studies at Conrad Grebel University College and author of *Ethics for Peacebuilders*

Contents

Introduction to The Jesus Way Series from Herald Press

The Jesus Way is good news for all people, of all times, in all places. Jesus Christ "is before all things, and in him all things hold together"; "in him all the fullness of God was pleased to dwell" (Colossians 1:17, 19). The Jesus Way happens when God's will is done on earth as it is in heaven.

But what does it mean to walk the Jesus Way? How can we who claim the name of Christ reflect the image of God in the twenty-first century? What does it mean to live out and proclaim the good news of reconciliation in Christ?

The Jesus Way: Small Books of Radical Faith offers concise, practical theology that helps readers encounter big questions about God's work in the world. Grounded in a Christ-centered reading of Scripture and a commitment to reconciliation, the series aims to enliven the service and embolden the witness of people who follow Jesus. The volumes in the series are written by a diverse community of internationally renowned pastors, scholars, and practitioners committed to the way of Jesus.

The Jesus Way series is rooted in Anabaptism, a Christian tradition that prioritizes following Jesus, loving enemies, and creating faithful communities. During the Protestant Reformation of the 1500s, early Anabaptists who began meeting for worship emphasized discipleship in addition to belief, baptized adults instead of infants, and pledged their allegiance to God over loyalty to the state. Early Anabaptists were martyred for their radical faith, and they went to their deaths without violently resisting their accusers.

Today more than two million Anabaptist Christians worship in more than one hundred countries around the globe. They include Mennonites, Amish, Brethren in Christ, and Hutterites. Many other Christians committed to Anabaptist beliefs and practices remain in church communities in other traditions.

Following Jesus means turning from sin, renouncing violence, seeking justice, believing in the reconciling power of God, and living in the power of the Holy Spirit. The Jesus Way liberates us from conformity to the world and heals broken places. It shines light on evil and restores all things.

Join Christ-followers around the world as we seek the Jesus Way.

Introduction

I was surrounded by four people who each held a broken bottle, ready to stab me if I made any quick moves. I was determined to fight, but suddenly . . .

This event occurred during my sophomore year of high school in Asunción, Paraguay. After a class meeting, I was heading to a bus stop. It was getting dark and there was a sprinkle of rain. A woman approached me and asked me for money for bus fare. I was happy to help and gave her some coins. As she reached for the coins, she suddenly touched my gold ring and asked me what it was. Something did not feel right, and I knew that I needed to leave this situation immediately. I was about to run, but it was too late. I could feel the sharp edge of a broken bottle, ready to stab me if I resisted. I looked around and realized that I was surrounded by four people, three women and one man, all of whom were in their early twenties. They were each holding a broken bottle, and the man's bottle was touching my back. I was determined to fight because, at that moment, I thought that was the only way to escape from the situation. I had some experience in Tae Kwon Do and had watched numerous martial arts movies, so I felt confident that I could beat these four people. I had my defense all planned out in my mind, but as I was about to execute it, an image passed through my mind. I saw myself lying down, slowing dying of excessive bleeding. In this image, I was apologizing to my mother for leaving her too soon.

After seeing this terrifying image, I did not know what to do next. A few milliseconds later, a Bible passage came to me: "If anyone wants to . . . take your coat, give your cloak as well" (Matthew 5:40). I knew then what I had to do. I immediately knelt, opened my backpack, and showed my attackers everything I had. I took out my wallet and gave them all the money. I also took off my ring and my shoes, and told them, in a gentle way, that these items were theirs. I noticed that these strangers were surprised by this unexpected response, and the man asked, "Why are you so nice?" What happened next surprised me as well. I thought that they would take everything, but they gave me back my wallet and ID, saying that I would need them. They also insisted that, since I was a student, it was crucial for me to have my backpack and my books. Because I was now barefoot, the man gave me his shoes. I had not anticipated this response, but before leaving me the man told me that he was sorry for robbing me and added that he was just following orders. I felt the sincerity of his words. I lost some personal belongings, but gained some important life lessons, especially about nonviolent engagement.

This book is about a Christian practice of nonviolence: how to love and engage with our enemies. The purpose of this book is not to incite guilt in those who do not practice pacifism or to argue that pacifists are morally superior people. Rather, the purpose of this book is to help readers better understand the Christian practice of nonviolence, how it relates to Christian discipleship, and how to apply it concretely in our contemporary daily life. As a follower of Jesus, I am a pacifist, and while I hope for everyone to become Christian pacifists, I do not expect that everyone will do so. However, I do believe that there are insights and wisdom that everyone can gain from the practice of nonviolence. For this reason, I want to invite every reader, whether pacifist or not and whether Christian or not, on this short journey where we will explore nonviolent engagement.

In chapter 1, we will begin by exploring how Jesus treated his enemies, as well as his teachings about the love of enemies. Chapter 2 examines how the practice of nonviolence is connected to faith and spiritual life. Chapter 3 observes closely the views of those who oppose pacifism, especially the views of Christians who are proponents of just war theory. Then, in chapter 4, we will examine the counterarguments to those who are part of the historic peace churches, and some of the fruitful outcomes from the debate between the two groups. Chapter 5 explores how nonviolence actually works in the public square and in society, and whether it is effective to bring about social transformation. To conclude, chapter 6 will look at the end goal of love of enemies and how nonviolence can be applied in our daily lives. Throughout the book, key terms appear in bold and are defined in the glossary.

This book does not aim to answer every question about a Christian practice of nonviolence, but it will help you deepen your faith and thought as you ponder how to live with your enemies in a violent world. I welcome you to this journey. With an open mind and heart, let us begin.

1

Who Were Jesus' Enemies?

Jesus was born in Palestine, whose history is marked by the presence of multiple empires, which each in turn conquered and exploited the inhabitants, particularly the Jews. During Jesus' time, the Roman Empire controlled the land and imposed unjust laws and heavy taxes, mercilessly hanging on crosses those who revolted against the empire. Within the limited freedom allowed by Rome, Israel's political sphere was governed by King Herod and his successors, and the religious sphere by the Pharisees, scribes, chief priests, and Sadducees. While there were some good and faithful leaders, the four gospels give witness to the reality that many of Israel's leaders during this time took advantage of their own people. The political leaders demanded high taxes in addition to the tax that the people were required to pay to the Roman Empire, and the religious leaders utilized their authority to force the people to follow numerous laws that even they themselves could not follow.

In this oppressive time and place, Jesus' life was threatened several times. Shortly after the visit of the wise men, King Herod sought to kill the baby Jesus (Matthew 2:16). In Luke 13, the Pharisees tell Jesus that Herod Antipas was planning to kill him. Luke 4:29 records an incident in which Jesus was almost pushed off a cliff. And we read about Pharisees, the chief priests, and the scribes seeking to conspire against Jesus and to destroy him (see Matthew 12:14; Mark 11:18). In the end, he was betrayed by one of his disciples, Judas Iscariot, and abandoned by the eleven disciples and the crowd of Jews whom he served. The religious leaders adamantly demanded that he be killed, Pontius Pilate condemned him to be crucified, and finally, the Roman soldiers tortured and executed him. He died at the hands of his enemies.

Carefully examining Jesus' attitude toward his enemies, theologian Gerard A. Vanderhaar states that Jesus demonstrated a mixture of courage and prudence. Jesus sometimes avoided dangerous encounters, and it was never his goal to antagonize Roman soldiers, but when he faced his enemies he did not flinch, while maintaining his dignity and remaining firm in his principles. He always respected each person and did not respond with self-defensive counter-aggression or escalate into a vicious cycle of violence.[1] Without a doubt, Jesus lived out what he taught about the love of enemies.

Jesus commanded his followers to love their enemies, both in Matthew 5 and Luke 6. These passages explain to us both *why* we need to love our enemies and *how* to love our enemies. Why do we need to love our enemies? The passages say that we are to love our enemies because we are God's children, and as God's children, we need to imitate our Father in heaven, who is "kind to the ungrateful and the wicked" (Luke 6:35) and who makes the "sun rise on the evil and on the good, and sends rain on the righteous and on the unrighteous" (Matthew 5:45). Jesus teaches us to love our enemies because we are God's children, and as children do, we imitate our parent. God our Father loves the ungrateful, the wicked, the evil, and the unrighteous just as God loves the good and the righteous. By treating people indiscriminately and treating our enemies with love, we participate in God's character.

It is important to note that Jesus is not telling us to love our enemies because, through loving them, we might convert our enemies or make a better world. Also, in these passages, Jesus does not differentiate between different types of enemies, such as political, national, military, familial, or religious enemies. When Jesus says to love our enemies, the word *enemies* encompasses all types of enemies.

HOW SHOULD WE TREAT OUR ENEMIES?

How exactly should we treat our enemies? Shouldn't they be treated differently from those who do good to us? Because Matthew 5 and Luke 6 have similar perspectives, rather than commenting on both passages, I will focus on Matthew 5, particularly verses 38-41.

A quick glance at Matthew 5 might lead us to believe that we should constantly make ourselves vulnerable to our enemies and allow them to commit abuse. But that is not what the passage is saying. In his book *Engaging the Powers*, Walter Wink helps us to understand this passage. In the second part of verse 39, Jesus says, "But if anyone strikes you on the right cheek, turn the other also." In order to understand this passage, we need to understand why Jesus specifically focuses on the right cheek. During Jesus' time, and as continues to be true in some contemporary cultures, greeting someone or touching them with one's left hand was prohibited because the left hand was used for unclean tasks. If the right hand was the only hand permitted for touching, then the only way to hit another person on the right cheek while facing them would be to use the back side of the right hand. Hitting one's enemy with the frontside of one's right hand on their right cheek would require twisting one's arm to an impossible angle. In Jesus' time, a person would slap another with the back of their right hand only if the other was considered to be of lower status. Masters gave backhanded slaps to their slaves, husbands to their wives, and parents to their children. This form of slapping was a physical punishment that reminded the person being slapped that they were of a lower status and should not dare to question or confront the authority of the one administering the punishment.

Jesus tells his listeners to turn the other cheek, meaning that they should turn their left cheek to their enemy. If a person turns their left cheek to someone who has just struck them, how might the perpetrator hit them a second time? Remember, the perpetrator cannot use their left hand, and cannot strike with a backhand blow of their right hand, because doing so would require twisting their arm. The only way to hit a second time is to use the fist or the open palm of the right, a method that was only used among people of equal status. Striking with one's fist indicated that the person striking and the one being struck were of the same status. By turning their left cheek, the person being struck is nonviolently challenging the perpetrator and refusing to be humiliated. Those who turn the other cheek are people who stand up for what they believe and invite a change of relationship.

Jesus gives another example, which takes place at court where a person is being sued for their outer garment. It is safe to assume that the person being sued is poor. Typically, a person's outer garment might be given as collateral for a loan, but would be the last possession one would hold on to. A person with nothing else to give up would be among the poorest of the poor. This situation would have been all too familiar to Jesus' listeners; the multiple layers of oppression they experienced left no option for poor people other than to become indebted in order to survive. However, Jesus tells the person being sued to offer their creditor not only their outer garment, but their inner garment as well, leaving them naked. Jesus knew that a poor person had no chance of winning such a court case, but offering both their outer and inner garments would create a scandalous situation, not for the naked debtor, but for the creditor who had obtained both garments. In Jesus' culture, nakedness was a scandal more for those seeing a naked body than for the person who was unclothed, and especially so for a person who forced another to become naked. According to Wink, this scandalous act would have caused shame for the creditor and revealed that the creditor is "not a legitimate moneylender but a party to the reduction of an entire social class to landlessness, destitution, and abasement. This unmasking is not simply punitive, therefore; it offers the creditor a chance to see, perhaps for the first time in his life, what his practices cause, and to repent."[2] Through this proactive action, Jesus invites us to find a different way of engaging the oppressor, one that refrains from using violence while maintaining our dignity.

A third example that Jesus gives involves going an extra mile for those who force you to go one mile. Roman soldiers were permitted to force Jews to carry a Roman soldier's load for one mile, but the law prohibited soldiers from forcing a person to carry their burden more than a mile because the

Roman authorities knew that if they imposed too great of a burden, the Jewish people would revolt. If a Jew refused to carry a Roman soldier's burden for a mile, that person could be punished, but if a Roman soldier demanded that a Jew carry his burden for more than a mile, it was the soldier who could be punished. Imagine if a solider demands that you return his load after you have carried his burden for a mile, but instead you willingly choose to continue walking. As a result, the soldier would become confused and anxious because he would know that he could be punished. Now the soldier would be pleading with you to return the load. Through this act, you reject being a victim but also free yourself from a vicious cycle of violence without using any violence.

Now, let's return to verse 38 and the first part of verse 39 of Matthew 5. Although Deuteronomy 19:21 teaches Israelites to "show no pity: life for life, eye for eye, tooth for tooth, hand for hand, foot for foot," Jesus believed that this was not what love looks like. Instead, Jesus instructs us to "not resist an evil-doer." The word that is translated as "resist" is *antistenai* in the original Greek language, which means to resist violently. Jesus is not saying to *not resist* but rather is saying to *not resist in a violent way*. Jesus follows this command with practical ways to resist nonviolently, and then commands us to love our enemies.

To conclude, through his life and teaching, Jesus tells us both *why* we should love our enemies and *how* to love them. When we are confronted by our enemies, it is our human inclination to choose between fighting or fleeing. Nonetheless, Jesus shows us an alternative way.

We are living in a different context from Jesus' time. There are no more Roman soldiers who demand that we carry loads, nor creditors suing for garments. We need to apply Jesus' teaching in our own context and to discern how we should live out a nonviolent alternative way of engagement with our enemies, oppressors, and perpetrators. Throughout this book, we will study how to concretely live out Jesus' teaching in our present world, a place that is still violent.

WE WERE ONCE GOD'S ENEMIES

According to the apostle Paul, we all were once God's enemies (Romans 5:10). When Paul wrote this, I have no doubt that he was reflecting on his past, in which he persecuted Christians. He says that, in God's eyes, all humans are sinners, and sinners are God's enemies. Nevertheless, Paul explains that God proved God's love for us "in that while we still were sinners Christ died for us" (Romans 5:8). While we were God's enemies, Jesus died for us to save and reconcile us with God. While we were living against God's will, Jesus showed his love toward us, his enemies. All who confess to be saved by Jesus have experienced this wonderous love. When Jesus commands us to love our enemies, he is asking us to love as people who have experienced this love of God. As we meditate on the love of enemy, it is crucial to remember that we were once God's enemies, but God loved us unconditionally and mercifully, and demonstrated on the cross how to love one's enemies. And because God still loves God's enemies, we who are God's children need to imitate God, which Jesus concretely showed how to do even while he was on a cross. Now the resurrected Jesus is calling all his followers to follow in his footsteps.

In the time of Jesus, there were many groups who continually sought opportunities to revolt against the Roman authorities. The Roman soldiers were waging war and looking for opportunities to expand their dominion. Whether fighting against oppressors or seeking to conquer the territories of others, they all had one common expression: "Take up the sword and fight." Amid this tumultuous time, Jesus proclaimed a countercultural approach, calling his followers to "take up your cross daily and follow me" (Luke 9:23), meaning that we should renounce our weapons and follow his way. Even after two thousand years, Jesus is still inviting us to that calling in our present world.

2

How Does Loving Enemies Connect to My Spiritual Life?

An Anabaptist martyr named Dirk Willems was burned outside the town of Asperen, Netherlands, on May 16, 1569. The *Martyrs Mirror* recounts his story:

> Dirk was caught, tried and convicted as an Anabaptist in those later years of harsh Spanish rule under the Duke of Alva in The Netherlands. He escaped from a residential palace turned into a prison by letting himself out of a window with a rope made of knotted rags, dropping onto the ice that covered the castle moat. Seeing him escape, a palace guard pursued him as he fled. Dirk crossed the thin ice of a pond, the "Hondegat," safely. His own weight had been reduced by short prison rations, but the heavier pursuer broke through. Hearing the guard's cries for help, Dirk turned back and rescued him. The less-than-grateful

Etching of Dirk Willems by Dutch artist Jan Luyken

guard then seized Dirk and led him back to captivity. This time the authorities threw him into a more secure prison, a small, heavily barred room at the top of a very tall church tower, above the bell, where he was probably locked into the wooden leg stocks that remain in place today. Soon he was led out to be burned to death.[1]

What is your reaction after reading this story? Do you see Willems's action as heroic or foolish? When I first heard this story, I had mixed feelings, Willems's decision to save the person who was pursing him was definitely an honorable act, but the story ends miserably. If the story had a different ending—for example, if the guard repented and became an

Anabaptist—then my reaction would have been different. But because we do not see any hint of repentance from the guard and we must face the reality that Willems was eventually killed, a part of me has always felt uncomfortable with this story. I was not excited about sharing it, especially with those who are not pacifists.

Nonetheless, Jesus reminds us that the love of enemies and nonviolence are done not because they promise a better result or because they are the best method to "convert" our enemies. Rather, we love our enemies and engage with them nonviolently because this is the way that Jesus taught us, and because, as children of God, it is one of the ways we participate in God's character. As a result, when we decide to follow Jesus, we do not calculate the best way to transform the world or measure the most efficient way to bring about our desired result; rather, we discern a faithful way of following Jesus' life and teachings. This means that loving our enemies and living nonviolently are rooted in our spiritual life and faith. In this chapter, I would like to explore more fully the relationship between the love of enemies and our spiritual life.

FEAR, TRUST, AND HUMILITY

Fear is a powerful emotion that influences how we react and think when we are faced with a perceived threat. Sometimes fear can be so overwhelming that our body simply shuts down, but much of the time fear helps us prepare to face a threat or escape from a dangerous situation by temporarily enhancing our focus and increasing our strength. When we sense fear, our brain quickly discerns whether a perceived threat is a real threat. This is why, according to psychiatrists Arash Javanbakht and Linda Saab, we respond differently when we see a lion in the wild versus in a zoo, or why we respond differently when someone is chasing us in a haunted house versus down a dark alley. Javanbakht and Saab argue that the way we react when we sense fear is based on "our sense of control."[2] The more we feel in control, the less we will feel threatened. Sometimes, if our sense of control is strong, we will even enjoy the thrill. The more we feel we are not in control, the more heightened our fight-or-flight response becomes. A sense of control is also central in Christian spirituality, and here is why.

Most people do not want to use violence as their first response to an enemy or a perceived threat. We try to find different ways to engage, but when we sense that there is no other option, or when we no longer have any sense of control, we choose violence because we believe that it will solve the problem of an immediate threat. Yet as Christians, instead of trying to take control of our lives, we are invited, as Proverbs 3:5-6 says, to "trust in the Lord with all your heart, and do not rely on your own insight. In all your ways acknowledge him, and he will make straight your paths." Likewise, just as Jesus did when he prayed in Gethsemane (Matthew 26:39), so in the Lord's Prayer we ask that the will of God, rather than our own will, be done.

Trusting in God does not mean giving up our reasoning and judgment. Instead, it means that we think critically and discern deeply but, in the end, trust that God is in control. In the Christian tradition, this kind of virtue is termed *humility*. Christian humility, as professor John Roth writes, asks us to have an active trust in God and our calling while we "adopt a posture of vulnerability and love in all circumstances, even when confronted by people who threaten us."[3] Humility asks us to surrender our desire to control through violence but, at the same time, to stand firm to our Christian conviction and calling. Humility is a posture that asks us to "love other people in the same way that God has loved us in Christ: non-coercively, gently, creatively, vulnerably, invitationally. Humility is the concrete embodiment of our confidence that God loves us and that God is in control of human history."[4]

It takes courage and risk to give up our sense of control and to trust in God's way. For this reason, love toward enemies and nonviolent engagement embody spiritual discipline. Giving up our desire to control and trusting God do not happen naturally and through brain power alone. Learning to trust God is a lifelong journey that requires intentional effort and a long period of discipline. Fear is a natural emotion, but seeking to discipline our sense of control is a profoundly spiritual endeavor.

EFFECTIVENESS VERSUS FAITHFULNESS

Some people justify the use of violence by arguing that violence is an effective method to stop an immediate danger and to bring about a quick solution. Proponents of this approach argue that to be a responsible citizen or a responsible leader, we sometimes need to use violence to strike against our enemies. Mennonite theologian John Howard Yoder challenges this discourse.[5] Yoder lists various motivations for pacifism, such as the value of human life, the belief that pacifism is a noble idea, and the belief that pacifism is the most effective way to bring changes.[6] Yet for the followers of Jesus, our commitment to and fundamental reason for nonviolence is that we want to be faithful to Jesus and to his teachings.[7] Consequently, love toward enemies is spiritual.

We confess that we do not know what result nonviolence will bring, but we engage in it because it is the way of the cross. Both the life of Jesus and the witness of Dirk Willems are examples of this way. Willems knew that he would not be rewarded for his act of kindness, but despite that, and because he was deeply committed to following the way of Jesus, he rescued his pursuer. This rescue happened in a split second; there was no time for Willems to measure and calculate how his act would benefit him or bring change in others. There was no time for hesitation. After hearing his pursuer shouting for help, Willems immediately turned and helped him. At the moment his fear was telling him to run, his spiritual life and discipline informed his actions and empowered him to reach out his hands to his enemy. He faithfully lived out what he believed and practiced.

In his book *Dissident Discipleship*, professor David Augsburger offers the following key characteristics of a spirituality of nonviolence:

> A spirituality of active nonviolence chooses faithfulness to the way of Jesus, the way of the cross, over personal security; chooses the practice of nonviolent love over defensive, reactive rage; rejects even regretfully or remorsefully resorting to violent self-defence as less than the spirituality of the cross.

> A spirituality of active nonviolence refuses to join the spiral of violence–retaliation–violence–revenge–violence–recrimination–violence–retribution.

> A spirituality of active nonviolence seeks a constructive process for addressing, resolving, and reconciling conflicts, and it seeks to transform the system that engendered the conflict in the first place.

> A spirituality of active nonviolence is an act of faith in the nonviolent God revealed to us in the nonresistant Jesus, who confronted evil with all his power but without abuse of power.

A spirituality of active nonviolence seeks the truth, the opponent's truth as well as its own; seeks genuine human social concern, believing that humans are meant to love and to be loved.

A spirituality of active nonviolence is a politics of repentance and reconciliation that works for transformation of broken systems, for healing of wounded persons, for change in the human order.

A spirituality of active nonviolence is not optimism about human conflict—it takes evil very seriously—but it believes in the reality of good even more than in the reality of evil.[8]

If we relinquish effectiveness as our goal, does that mean we need to follow Jesus blindly? No. Living out the love of enemies is a proactive method of following Jesus with all our strength, soul, and *mind*, but when it comes to deciding who is in control and how we will engage with our enemies, we trust that God is in control and that we engage with our enemies nonviolently. We do this because it is the way that Jesus has revealed to us and because we believe that Jesus knows much better than we do how to engage with enemies. We do so because this response is a participation in God's character and because we believe that God knows what is best for us, more than anyone else in this universe, since God is our creator and our final judge.

I want to summarize the spirituality of nonviolence by offering the image of the two hands of nonviolence, an image that was first introduced by the late activist and writer Barbara Deming. One hand is lifted strongly and is signaling the enemy to stop. The gesture of this hand indicates that I stand against your wrong deed or oppressive act, I am not participating in it, and I am going to do everything I can, except use violence, to stop you. At the same time, the other hand is outstretched graciously, indicating that I will never give up on you, that I will continually love you, and that I believe you are valuable as well. This image captures Jesus' call to seek to actively stop violence without using violence, and to always be reaching out to offer love.

MORE THAN ENEMIES

Before ending this chapter, I would like to delve a bit deeper into defining our enemies. Although we have come to this chapter assuming we all have enemies, as Christians, do we really have enemies other than Satan? How do we define *enemy*? According to the *Oxford English Dictionary*, an enemy is one "that cherishes hatred, that wishes or seeks to do ill to another."[9] In this world, undeniably, there are people who actively oppose or are hostile to one another. There are people who cause violence and oppress us, and we may define them as our enemies. But what would happen if we stopped defining them as enemies? If we actively reject labeling them only as enemies, that does not mean we ignore the pain and suffering they are causing, but it does mean that we must engage with them differently.

I do not believe that there is any human being who is born to be my enemy. There may be people with a certain character and attitude that I dislike, but no one is born to be my lifelong enemy. Rather, enemies are made through several factors, whether through a small mistake, through a misinterpretation of my actions, by social factors like racism, or through national actions such as a war between our countries. Most of the time, enemies are made through our unexamined imaginings and information about our "enemies." When we carefully start examining why certain people are our enemies, and what information and imaginings are driving us to think that they are enemies, we will realize that our information and imaginings are not fully accurate, and we slowly begin to see these others as more than our "enemies."

When we begin to realize that God's image is also in our enemies, and that Jesus died for them as well, we will know that they are not merely enemies. Before his death, Jesus shouted out to God to forgive those who tortured him because "they do not know what they are doing" (Luke 23:34). Stephen prayed a similar prayer, "Lord, do not hold this sin against them" (Acts 7:60), when he was being stoned by his persecutors. Both Jesus and Stephen confronted their oppressors, but they prayed for their persecutors before their death. I am convinced that Jesus and Stephen did not see their oppressors only as their enemies. I do not think Dirk Willems saw the guard only as his enemy. They all saw that the persecutors needed forgiveness, needed to know the truth, and needed to be helped and saved. They saw their oppressors through God's eyes, and they imitated God's character. They rejected seeing their perpetrators as merely enemies.

3

Isn't Violence Sometimes Necessary?

Imagine that you are on your balcony and you see a stranger who is carrying a gun and is about to climb over your neighbor's wall and enter their main door. You have a gun. As a Christian, how will you practice neighborly love? If you truly love your neighbor, won't you use violence to stop the stranger in order to protect your neighbor? Isn't that love? Isn't that being a responsible neighbor?

This is a scenario that is often cited by proponents of **just war theory**. Just war theory, which I will explain in more depth later on, is a belief that war and violence can be justified in specific situations, and that defines how violence can legitimately be used. Those who believe in just war theory argue that loving our neighbor means protecting our neighbor as much as possible, even if that requires giving up our pious life by using violence. This argument was originally made by

Augustine of Hippo, a bishop in North Africa in 396–430 and the founder of just war theory in the Christian tradition.

Neighborly love does mean protecting the weak and the vulnerable, but the argument behind this scenario is based on two flawed presuppositions. First, it limits the definition of a neighbor to the person who physically lives beside my house. What about the attacker? Is not the stranger a neighbor from a Christian perspective? Is not the stranger also created in God's image, someone for whom Jesus died? Second, the scenario assumes that, in using the gun, I would be able to stop the stranger from injuring my neighbor. But there is no guarantee that by obtaining and using a gun, I would be able to save my neighbor. By showing up with a gun, I may intensify the situation, and everyone may end up getting killed. In that case, would it not be better to engage nonviolently by calming the stranger?

Christian pacifists argue that there is no justification for using violence, while Christian proponents of just war theory argue that violence is sometimes needed to stop a greater evil, although they agree with pacifists that violence should never be the first means of response. It is important to clarify here that Christian pacifists differentiate between coercive force and lethal violence. While all Christian pacifists are against the use of violence, some pacifists believe that using coercive force can be fine and necessary as long as it does not cause death. They acknowledge that it is hard to draw a line between coercive force and lethal violence, yet believe that there is a fundamental difference between them.

THE MYTH OF REDEMPTIVE VIOLENCE

Can violence truly overcome evil and lead us to a better society and world? Walter Wink argues that the **myth of redemptive**

violence is deeply rooted in Western society. This myth is a belief that, even though we acknowledge that violence is a terrible thing and believe that we should avoid it as much as possible, it is ultimately a necessary evil to fight against even greater evils and to protect our civilized and good society. This myth is widely accepted in our society, and appears frequently in popular culture, from cartoons to movies, and from everyday conversations to our history books.

Whether you are a fan of Marvel or DC superhero movies, their plotlines are quite similar. Typically, the main characters do not want to use their superpower, and some even abhor using their power. They try hard to blend in with normal people, but most of the time they fail. One day villains appear, disrupting the lives of innocent people, and the superheroes have no option but to use force. At first they are extremely careful in using their force so that they do not kill the villains, but there comes a moment of crisis in which, if the superheroes do not destroy the villains, the lives of many beloved people will soon end. After several hesitations and finding no alternative, the heroes finally destroy the villains. As a result, the whole town or even the whole world is saved. The rescued people thank the heroes for risking everything to save them, and no one criticizes the heroes for using lethal force. Because violence has been used to protect, and especially to protect weak and innocent people, it is not only justified but also praised. We can see that the myth of redemptive violence is deeply seated in these movies.

The myth of redemptive violence can also be found in our understanding of national history. When we read about the American Civil War, World War I, World War II, the Korean War, and other wars, we hear stories about nations that had no option other than fighting to protect their freedom, their rights, and their people. Noticing how this myth is widespread and deeply rooted, Wink writes, "If a god is what you turn to when all else fails, violence certainly functions as a god. What people overlook, then, is the religious character of violence. It demands from its devotees an absolute obedience-unto-death."[1]

The myth of redemptive violence is based on several assumptions, one of which is that violence can bring an end to an escalating conflict and is a final solution to all problems. But Jesus says that "all who take the sword will perish by the sword" (Matthew 26:52), meaning that violence begets violence. As we can observe, the more the United States tries to eradicate terrorist groups through direct military intervention, the more it creates hatred against itself and fuels terrorist attacks. Another assumption of the myth of redemptive violence is that whatever we are seeking to protect through violence is more important than the lives of those who may be destroyed in the process. Thus, in order to protect our rights, our freedom, our beliefs, our religions, our possessions, our ideologies, our cultures, we destroy the others. There is nothing Christlike about these assumptions.

JUST WAR THEORY

Wink argues that just war theory is a Christian appropriation of the myth of redemptive violence. I agree to a degree, although I also see that argument as an oversimplification. Just war theory has a long history in the Christian tradition, starting with Augustine of Hippo, and has evolved through the centuries. Although the logic of the myth of redemptive violence can be identified within just war theory, I am also aware of just war theologians who have wrestled with the theme of violence, the complexity of human lives, the sinful nature of humanity, issues of social justice, and the complicated relationship between the church and the state. For this reason, I do not want to quickly dismiss just war theory as a Christian appropriation of the myth of redemptive violence. The Roman Catholic Church, which is one of the Christian denominations that holds to just war theory, strongly encourages a personal commitment to nonviolence and forbids using lethal force on the innocent. For this reason, the Catholic Church opposes abortion and euthanasia. However, when a state goes to war or uses violent force, as a church community, the church leaders discern whether the use of violence of the state is justified or not based on a list of criteria for a just war. This effort restricts the use of violence as much as possible. It is important to note that justice is a key criterion. If violence is inevitable, the church then argues that it should be used responsibly and justly. The Roman Catholic Church criteria is divided into two categories—"justice before war" and "justice during war"—in Latin, *jus ad bellum* and *jus in bello*.

Justice before war (*jus ad bellum*):

- *Just cause:* Force may be used only to correct a grave, public evil.
- *Comparative justice:* To override the presumption against the use of force the injustice suffered by one party must significantly outweigh that suffered by the other.
- *Legitimate authority:* Only duly constituted public authorities may use deadly force.
- *Right intention:* Force may be used only in a truly just cause and solely for that purpose.
- *Probability of success:* Arms may not be used in a futile cause or in a case where disproportionate measures are required to achieve success.
- *Proportionality:* The destruction expected from the use of force must be outweighed by the good to be achieved.

- *Last resort:* Force may be used only after all peaceful alternatives have been tried and exhausted.

Justice during war (*jus in bello*):

- *Noncombatant immunity:* Civilians may not be the object of direct attack, and military personnel must take due care to minimize indirect harm to civilians.
- *Proportionality:* Efforts must be made to attain military objectives with no more force than is militarily necessary and to avoid disproportionate collateral damage to civilian life and property.
- *Right intention:* The aim of political and military leaders must be peace with justice, so that acts of vengeance and indiscriminate violence are forbidden.[2]

The list has been updated, and it will continue to evolve as human society changes. Although the Roman Catholic Church officially permits the use of lethal force, this does not mean that all Catholics are proponents of just war theory. There are Roman Catholics who are advocates for pacifism; some of the most well-known include Thomas Merton, John Dear, Dorothy Day, and Mother Teresa.

Like any theory, just war theory is not without criticism. One main criticism is that since the time of Augustine until the present, just war theory has never been applied. While the proponents of just war theory criticize pacifism as too ideal, their position seems idealistic as well. As a pacifist, I do not agree with the principles of just war theory, but if they could be kept and truly practiced, that would be acceptable to me. While I advocate for Christians to be pacifist, I also encourage the proponents of just war theory to live out the principles they embrace. I believe that if the principles are truly applied, the use of violence will decrease exponentially.

Priest John Dear rightly stated that from a Christian perspective, "if ever there was a moment when just war theory
might apply, when violence would be divinely sanctioned
and justified, it's in that garden scene moments before Jesus
is arrested and hauled off to his execution. This one moment
stands as the ultimate point in history in which violence could
have been applied."[3] Everyone knew that Jesus was an innocent and righteous person, and Peter had every reason to fight
for him. Yet Jesus tells Peter to "put your sword back into its
place" (Matthew 26:52). Peter was eager to protect his mas-
ter, the Christ, the Messiah, the Son of the living God. But
Jesus' command to Peter was to put down the sword because
Jesus knew that violence begets violence. Jesus did not want to
build God's kingdom on the myth of redemptive violence. He
wanted to build the kingdom through love and nonviolence.
It is so hard for us to accept and understand this because the
myth of redemptive violence is so prevalent and deeply seated
in our cultural DNA and imagination—in fact, in the whole
human society. Nevertheless, the resurrected Jesus has been
creating a new reality and is inviting us to live into this new
way of life. Now it is up to us whether we will accept this
new way.

4

Do Christian Pacifists Exist among Us?

Maximilian was the son of a Roman soldier. At age twenty-one he is brought to court and ordered to be enrolled as a soldier—such is the law of the empire. "I refuse to accept military service," he said. "My army is the army of God, and I cannot fight for this world." Dio, the proconsul, or governor, of the region, notes correctly that many Christians are serving the empire. "That is their business," says Maximilian. "I am a Christian too, and I cannot serve." Dio tells the father to correct his son. "He knows what he believes, and he won't change his mind," says the father, whose name is lost. . . . Dio tells Maximilian that he will die unless he changes his mind. "I shall not die," says Maximilian. "When I leave this earth I shall live with Christ." Dio sentences him to death. He says farewell to his friends and to his father, and he is beheaded. His father, say the annals, went home joyfully, thanking God for having allowed him to send such a gift to heaven.[1]

There is ongoing debate about whether early Christians were pacifists. According to the current scholarship, it seems that not all Christians were pacifists, as is evident from this dialogue between Dio and Maximilian in 295 CE. Yet there is ample evidence that the first Christians were almost entirely pacifists, and there were numerous Christian pacifists even after the time of Maximilian. While Christian pacifists are not widely visible and known in larger society, they have existed from the time of Jesus, and a vibrant stream of Christian pacifism continues to exist. In particular, the churches that have an official long-standing commitment to pacifism and nonviolence are called the **historic peace churches**. The three main churches represented among the historic peace churches are the Mennonites, the Church of the Brethren, and the Religious Society of Friends, or Quakers. While there are other churches committed to nonviolence, these three denominations became known as the historic peace churches after they held a meeting in Kansas in 1935 to address their concern about wars that were happening around that time. They intentionally named themselves "historic" because their commitment to peace was not a recent decision because of special circumstances; rather, they had always been committed to peace from the beginning of their existence.

Two of these three denominations, the Mennonites and the Church of the Brethren, have the same root—the Anabaptist movement, which dates back to the sixteenth-century Protestant Reformation. Anabaptists believed that the Reformation did not go far enough, and advocated for more radical changes, such as separation between the church and the state. Since Anabaptists firmly believed that baptism must be voluntary and occur only when one is old enough to make a conscious decision, they opposed baptizing infants. As a symbol of their dedication to fully following Jesus as adults and an acknowledgment that their infant baptism was not valid, they rebaptized themselves. As a result, they were called Anabaptist, which means "re-baptizers" (the Greek *ana* means "again"), a term that was originally a derogatory nickname used against them. Some contemporary Mennonites and Brethren prefer to be called Anabaptists because they do not want to limit their faith identity and community to one denomination or to their ethnic and cultural identity.

Another central belief of the Anabaptists is seriously seeking to practice Jesus' teaching in the Sermon on the Mount. Traditionally, Roman Catholics interpret the teaching from the Sermon on the Mount as applying to only a few committed Christian leaders, like priests and nuns. Some Protestant groups perceive that Jesus' teachings in the Sermon on the Mount are not achievable, so they only emphasize God's grace. Anabaptists believe that all adult believers are called to live out the Sermon on the Mount, and since Jesus' teaching on the love of enemy is part of that teaching, they wholeheartedly try to live a nonviolent life. From the beginning of the Anabaptist movement up through contemporary times, Anabaptists have lived out this commitment. Throughout history, they have faced severe challenges. In the beginning, they were persecuted both by the Roman Catholics and by Protestant groups. They endured the Thirty Years' War, the American Revolution, the American Civil War, and World Wars I and II. On each occasion, Anabaptists were pressured to choose sides or to participate in war, but many, although not all, maintained their commitment to nonviolence. Some did abandon their nonviolent stance, and some even willingly joined in wars, but overall, the Anabaptists maintained their commitment to peace and nonviolence.

HISTORIC PEACE CHURCHES' RESPONSES TO WAR

One might ask, since the historic peace churches are pacifists, do they merely remain passive and oppose war? Well, no. The historic peace churches have developed several statements and specific actions to respond actively to war. For example, the Mennonite Brethren Church has issued the following guidelines:

Some Christian responses to war

1. Pray for peace and for people in government.
2. Make every effort to obey the law; however, do not accept military service which involves training in how to kill fellow human beings who are also made in the image of God.
3. Join a relief organization to serve unarmed in war zones; provide aid to the victims of war.
4. Do not avoid dangerous assignments while doing good; Christians are not cowards.
5. Even in honorable professions and businesses, do not exploit the tragedy of war for personal gain.
6. Make a living by producing goods and services that sustain life; refuse jobs associated with killing and destruction.
7. Be willing to accept the penalties which the state may impose for those who refuse to participate in military action.
8. Witness to the conviction that Christians who believe that Jesus taught his followers not to kill cannot serve as soldiers but willingly serve their country in constructive ways.
9. Urge the peaceful resolution of all disputes while recognizing that leaders of countries are part of this

world's system and do not, therefore, rule in full accord with the biblical principle of peace.

10.   Share the good news of salvation even in time of war.[2]

It is easy to misinterpret Christian pacifists as people who only oppose war and do not take seriously their responsibility as citizens of their own countries. But as one can see in this statement, pacifists are committed to active nonviolent engagement and participation in society.

Christian pacifism can also be misinterpreted as a conviction that is limited to the issue of war, but from the perspective of the historic peace churches, nonviolence is a way of life. The *Confession of Faith in a Mennonite Perspective* states, "Led by the Spirit, and beginning in the church, we witness to all people that violence is not the will of God. We witness against all forms of violence, including war among nations, hostility among races and classes, abuse of children and women, violence between men and women, abortion, and capital punishment."[3] In other words, a commitment to nonviolence and pacifism is about standing against all forms of violence that exist in human life and relationships. Peace encompasses all areas of human life. A commitment to peace involves standing against racism, opposing sexism, and being in solidarity with the weak and with marginalized people. A commitment to peace involves fighting against hunger and poverty and working for the social welfare of all people. It also includes creating a culture of peace, advocating for human rights, and being involved in relief work. In chapter 6, we will examine this area more thoroughly.

Just as there are differing opinions among Roman Catholics about the use of violence, there are also different perspectives on nonviolence among Christian pacifists. For instance, on one end of the spectrum, there are Mennonites who forbid any kind of coercive force, and on the other end there are some who argue that policing to maintain order is acceptable. There are some Mennonite scholars who are reluctant to have absolute nonviolence as a norm in every situation because each context is different. They argue that we cannot be completely sure that nonviolence is the only way to solve all conflicts. Their stance does not mean that they want to compromise their Mennonite faith, but it means that they want to leave their peace position open to listen to and dialogue with other perspectives.

JUST PEACEMAKING

Are the proponents of just war and pacifism always opposed? Has there been any fruitful result from dialogue between these groups? As a result of several dialogues, these two groups seem to be moving closer together. The proponents of just war are working hard to have a more restrictive use of violence. Some proponents choose to be selective conscientious objectors (being conscientious objectors only in certain wars that seem to be unjust), and others are nuclear pacifists (a position that a nuclear war cannot be just). And some pacifists are becoming more open to certain forms of policing, while others have come to reject absolute pacifism. In addition, many Christian pacifists acknowledge that the use of violence is inevitable in society and by the state. Most importantly, the proponents of just war and pacifism have come to agree on and work together for a third paradigm, called **just peacemaking**.

The just peacemaking paradigm emerged because the dialogue between pacifism and just war theory seemed to be focused on war, and not on practices that could prevent conflicts from escalating into war. This became a more urgent agenda as several countries began to accumulate weapons of mass destruction. After several discussions among scholars and activists from various Christian traditions and fields of study, ten practices of just peacemaking were developed and are now widely accepted by many Christian communities, denominations, and organizations, as well as by other religious groups, including some Jewish and Muslim communities. The ten practices are:

1. Support nonviolent direct action.
2. Take independent initiatives to reduce threat.
3. Use cooperative conflict resolution.
4. Acknowledge responsibility for conflict and injustice.
5. Advance democracy, human rights, and interdependence.
6. Foster just and sustainable economic development.
7. Work with emerging cooperative forces in the international system.
8. Strengthen the United Nations and international efforts for cooperation and human rights.
9. Reduce offensive weapons and weapons trade.
10. Encourage grassroots peacemaking groups and voluntary associations.[4]

As one can tell, the advantage of this paradigm is that both groups—pacifists and proponents of just war theory—can work together to prevent war. This approach contains perspectives and elements from both traditions. It includes the realism of just war and the pacifists' commitment to nonviolence. Another advantage of this paradigm is that it invites a wider range of people to participate. Usually, with the issue of war, the dialogue is conducted among high government officials and experts, but even grassroots people can contribute to just peacemaking. Historians and political scientists have determined that these practices actually work to prevent war.

One can ask if the just peacemaking paradigm can replace pacifism and just war theory. Christian ethicist Glen Stassen held that just peacemaking is not guaranteed to prevent all wars. If just peacemaking fails and a war is about to occur, we still will have to decide whether it is right to make war or whether we should commit to nonviolence.[5] Because of this, the debate between pacifism and just war still needs to continue.

In Isaiah 2, we see a beautiful vision and prophecy. The writer says that all nations will stream to the house of the Lord and learn *God's ways* so that we may walk in *God's paths*. With these new ways, God will judge between the nations and mediate many peoples. As a result of this, people will "beat their swords into plowshares, and their spears into pruning hooks; nation shall not lift up sword against nation, neither shall they learn war any more" (Isaiah 2:4). Some interpreters understand this passage to depict a vision that will become a reality when God judges and restores all creation in the last day. I agree, but also believe, as do the historic peace churches, that *God's ways* and *God's paths* were revealed and taught by Jesus. Therefore, Jesus' teaching of the love of enemies and nonviolence is not to be practiced only in the last day, but rather here and now. This is how the young Maximilian lived out his belief.

5

Does Loving Our Enemies Really *Work*?

I see that nonviolence can work in an interpersonal relationship and in a church community, but does it realistically
work in society and the world? Can it really work to bring
social transformation? I get that the love of enemy is about
faithfulness and not about effectiveness, but it sounds too
ideal and unrealistic.

I understand that some of you might be asking these questions. For this reason, I have dedicated this chapter to exploring the effectiveness of nonviolence. "What?" you might be
interjecting. In chapter 2, I said that the love of enemies is
about faithfulness and not effectiveness. Faithfulness does
need to be the foundation of Christian pacifism, but at the
same time, nonviolence can be effective. But before we explore
the effectiveness of nonviolence, I want to clarify two terms
that I have used interchangeably.

PACIFISM AND NONVIOLENCE

So far, I have used the words *pacifism* and *nonviolence* synony-
mously because they are similar in many aspects. However, the
words have different origins and sometimes are used to refer
to different aspects of the same concept. The word *pacifism* is
originally from a French word, *pacifisme*, and literally means
"love of peace," or "committed to peace." An appropriately
broad meaning of pacifism includes one's commitment to the
work of peace, but the word is often used in a narrower way
to refer only to opposition to war. While the concept of nonviolence existed prior to Mahatma Gandhi, he was the first person to articulate it clearly as the only way to bring about genuine social transformation. Gandhi is responsible for helping to
popularize the concept by successfully achieving India's independence from the British Empire. **Nonviolence** is an active
resistance to bring social and political change without using
violence. It is usually used in the context of a campaign that
seeks social change or revolution. Because of these nuances,
pacifism and nonviolence are distinct. While some people are
pacifist and are committed to using nonviolent methods to
bring social change, not all pacifists are proponents of nonviolence, and vice versa. Some pacifists do not agree with nonviolent methods, because some nonviolent methods are open to
the use of force to pressure government and institutions. And
some proponents of nonviolence are open to joining a war
when the war is just.

Although the concepts of pacifism and nonviolence are distinct, from a Christian tradition, they are both rooted in Jesus'
teaching of loving the enemy. Even before the words *pacifism*
and *nonviolence* existed, the love ethic of Jesus was central
for Christians. In time, some Christians adopted the term and
concept of pacifism and, much later, that of nonviolence. The

love ethic of Jesus was not and is not limited to applications in a context of war or of social change. Rather, this ethic needs to be applied in any area where one has to relate with one's enemies and oppressors, whether it is in an interpersonal relationship or the relationship between groups and communities.

EFFECTIVENESS OF NONVIOLENCE

Does loving enemies work? Does nonviolence work? In short, yes, nonviolence works, but it does not guarantee one hundred percent success. From history, we learn of the success of Gandhi's independence movement and the way it forged a path to freedom. We also learn how Martin Luther King Jr. and the nonviolent civil rights movement transformed American society. The documentary series A Force More Powerful features other successful nonviolent movements around the world in the twentieth century, which include the anti-apartheid movement in South Africa, the Danish resistance to Nazi occupation, the Polish Solidarity movement, and the Chilean democracy movement to overthrow dictator Augusto Pinochet. There are many more successful nonviolent resistance movements around the world, and still more to unearth from world history.

To see whether nonviolence really works, Harvard political scientist Erica Chenoweth and Maria Stephan of the U.S. Institute of Peace studied more than three hundred nonviolent and violent campaigns around the world between 1990 and 2006. They present what they have learned in the book *Why Civil Resistance Works: The Strategic Logic of Nonviolent Conflict.* When Chenoweth began this research, she thought that she would discover more successful cases of violent campaigns than nonviolent ones, but to her surprise, nonviolent resistance movements proved to be twice as likely to reach full or partial success as violent campaigns. Chenoweth and Stephan conclude that we are seeing more and more successful cases of nonviolent campaigns as opposed to violent ones.

In their research, Chenoweth and Stephan also analyzed why nonviolence is so effective. One of the main reasons they found is that nonviolence allows mass participation. In an armed struggle, only a few people who have the capacity to fight can join in, which is typically a small number of people. Since a nonviolent campaign is not as physically demanding as a violent struggle and seeks to welcome as many people as possible, children, elders, and a variety of people are able to join the movement. As a result, nonviolent movements attract a large number of participants who have similar yearnings. The larger the mass of participants, the higher the rate of success. Chenoweth and Stephan discovered that no campaign failed "once they'd achieved the active and sustained participation of just 3.5 percent of the population—and lots of them succeeded with far less than that. . . . Every single campaign that did surpass that 3.5 percent threshold was a nonviolent one."[1] Once a mass of 3.5 percent of the population joins the movement, it is certain that there will be people who are connected to security forces, the media, business, government, and other important institutions. And since no government exists in isolation from the population itself, a mass movement with all those connections has enough power to undermine the current authority and push toward social transformation.

Even if nonviolent movements do not succeed all the time, it is better to have nonviolent struggles than violent ones because of the long-term impact. Chenoweth asserts that "nonviolent campaigns were far more likely to usher in democratic institutions than violent insurgencies. And countries where people waged nonviolent struggles were 15 percent less likely to relapse into civil war."[2] Although a violent campaign might seem to bring an immediate solution, in the long run, it is not as effective as a nonviolent one.

There are critics who say that a nonviolent campaign succeeds only where government officials and soldiers have a moral code that does not allow them to kill innocent civilians, and will not work in a place where the top leaders have no such code, as in the cases of Hitler, Stalin, and Kim Jong Un. Yet the research done by Chenoweth and Stephan shows that nonviolence has worked and can work even in harsh, oppressive societies. Although a nonviolent campaign seeks to move and change the minds and hearts of oppressive leaders, it also seeks to win the sympathy of the masses and of third parties, inviting them to no longer be complicit with oppressive leaders and to join the movement for change. When these people finally join, this shift destabilizes the power base of the oppressors. Thus, a nonviolent campaign does not entirely depend on the moral code of the oppressive leaders to achieve its goal.

As several nonviolent activists argue, nonviolence itself does not bring success. Careful planning and strategy are needed to increase the chances of success; the key is in attaining mass mobilization and the cooperation of third parties. We can see this in the work of Martin Luther King Jr. As he integrated his belief in love of enemies, his understanding that nonviolence is the only solution to overcoming oppressive forces, and his realism about the ways that social change occurs, King developed six essential steps for any nonviolent social change:

1. *Information gathering:* To understand and articulate an issue, problem or injustice facing a person, community, or institution you must do research. You must investigate and gather all vital information from all sides of the argument or issue so as to increase your

understanding of the problem. You must become an expert on your opponent's position.

2. *Education:* It is essential to inform others, including your opposition, about your issue. This minimizes misunderstandings and gains you support and sympathy.

3. *Personal commitment:* Daily check and affirm your faith in the philosophy and methods of nonviolence. Eliminate hidden motives and prepare yourself to accept suffering, if necessary, in your work for justice.

4. *Discussion/negotiation:* Using grace, humor and intelligence, confront the other party with a list of injustices and a plan for addressing and resolving these injustices. Look for what is positive in every action and statement the opposition makes. Do not seek to humiliate the opponent but to call forth the good in the opponent.

5. *Direct action:* These are actions taken when the opponent is unwilling to enter into, or remain in, discussion/negotiation. These actions impose a "creative tension" into the conflict, supplying moral pressure on your opponent to work with you in resolving the injustice.

6. *Reconciliation:* Nonviolence seeks friendship and understanding with the opponent. Nonviolence does not seek to defeat the opponent. Nonviolence is directed against evil systems, forces, oppressive policies, unjust acts, but not against persons. Through reasoned compromise, both sides resolve the injustice with a plan of action. Each act of reconciliation is one step closer to the "Beloved Community."3

King offered concrete steps toward nonviolent engagement and for choosing nonviolent direct actions. Did you know that there are at least 198 different methods? In his three-volume book *The Politics of Nonviolent Action*, political scientist Gene Sharp identifies 198 methods of nonviolent action that have been used at different times in world history. You can also find the list online at Albert Einstein Institution's website.[4] Not all methods listed may be right for you. Some methods may seem too extreme or too aggressive. Each person should discern wisely which strategies and methods are appropriate for their group to utilize to challenge oppressive leaders and to invite the masses to join in their campaign. Also, the list does not need to end at 198 methods. We can continually find new, creative ways to engage nonviolently as we practice love of enemies and active engagement. Most importantly, whatever strategies and methods we choose, we should be aware that it takes great patience and persistence to bring about change.

While nonviolent campaigns are more successful and create less harm, sacrifice and suffering on the part of those participating in campaigns are inevitable. Consequently, nonviolent action requires courage and strength. Nonviolence does not praise suffering per se, because suffering itself is not noble or redemptive. Still, when one challenges repressive authority and engages in political struggle, suffering, sacrifice, and even death cannot be avoided. But as Sharp points out, when oppressors use violence, they are showing their weakness and desperation, and when the nonviolent resisters refuse to retaliate through violence, they are showing strength.[5] He also asserts that sacrifice and suffering are necessary only until mass noncooperation weakens the adversary's power.[6] Until then, one should continue to endure the burden with perseverance.

As I explained in the beginning of this chapter, not all nonviolent activists are pacifists. I also need to clarify that not all pacifists and nonviolent activists are Christian or religious people. Atheists have actively participated in numerous nonviolent campaigns, and their help has been crucial in achieving victory and success. Hearing this, one can then ask if faith or spiritual discipline is necessary to be a pacifist, nonviolent activist, and to practice the love of enemies. This is a good question, and one that I will answer in an indirect way.

When nonviolent action fails and there is too much pain and suffering to bear in the course of peace witnessing, you need something greater than yourself to guide you through the journey. When oppression continues for several generations and when you do not see the fruit of your labor in your life-time, you need a big picture to continually have hope. In this circumstance, one is tempted in every way to pick up a lethal weapon, and one's patience can run out pretty quickly, but in order to continue to love our enemies, we need to have a solid conviction that the One who knows everything and loves us so much wants us to take this path. In Christian language, one needs an unshakable faith in the teaching of Jesus, as well as hope that, somehow, God will transform all oppression and injustice. It was this faith that sustained Jesus, Maximilian, and Dirk Willems throughout their trials. The disciplines of social science and political science are accepting more and more the concept of nonviolence and advocating for it as a far more effective way to bring social transformation than vio-lence. Despite that, living out the love of enemies is not based on the scientific studies, although they definitely help. Rather, living out the love of enemies is based on being faithful to the teaching of Jesus and trusting that God will soon reconcile all things.

6

Nonviolence for What?

I have a dream that one day this nation will rise up and live out the true meaning of its creed: "We hold these truths to be self-evident: that all men are created equal."

I have a dream that one day on the red hills of Georgia the sons of former slaves and the sons of former slave owners will be able to sit down together at the table of brotherhood.

I have a dream that one day even the state of Mississippi, a state sweltering with the heat of injustice, sweltering with the heat of oppression, will be transformed into an oasis of freedom and justice.

I have a dream that my four little children will one day live in a nation where they will not be judged by the color of their skin but by the content of their character. I have a dream today.

I have a dream that one day, down in Alabama, with its vicious racists, with its governor having his lips dripping with the words of interposition and nullification; one day right there in Alabama, little black boys and black girls will be able to join hands with little white boys and white girls as sisters and brothers. I have a dream today.

I have a dream that one day every valley shall be exalted, every hill and mountain shall be made low, the rough places will be made plain, and the crooked places will be made straight, and the glory of the Lord shall be revealed, and all flesh shall see it together.[1]

This is a portion of Martin Luther King Jr.'s speech at the March on Washington for Jobs and Freedom on August 28, 1963. In his speech, we can see that King envisioned a new reality, a new way that people would relate to each other, and especially oppressors and the oppressed. His ultimate desire was for the **beloved community**. King stated, "The aftermath of nonviolence is the creation of the beloved community; so that when the battle's over, a new relationship comes into being between the oppressed and the oppressor."[2]

King knew that this beloved community cannot be achieved through violence, but is achieved only through nonviolence. For this reason, the goal of nonviolence is not about punishing, humiliating, or defeating our enemies and oppressors, but about working toward reconciliation, toward a new relationship, toward creating the beloved community. A nonviolent campaign seeks to set both the oppressor and the oppressed free.

I am confident that King's vision of the beloved community emerged from the concept of shalom in the Old Testament. According to prominent Old Testament scholar Walter Brueggemann, **shalom** is "the central vision of world history in the Bible . . . that all of creation is one, every creature in community with every other, living in harmony and security toward the joy and well-being of every other creature. . . . It bears tremendous freight—the freight of a dream of God that resists all our tendencies to division, hostility, fear, drivenness, and misery."[3] Shalom becomes a reality when we find peace between God and among people, nature, and ourselves. This vision of shalom is essentially the kingdom of God that Jesus has announced and begun! Since shalom and the kingdom are God's desire and plan, they have to be fulfilled in a way that aligns with God's heart and character, which calls for loving the ungrateful, the wicked, the evil, and the unrighteous as one loves the good and the righteous. Jesus knew about this truth, and so he lived it out and taught his disciples to love their enemies.

In building the beloved community, two fundamental elements are necessary: love and justice. A well-known maxim says, "There is no peace without justice." Peace is not sustainable without justice. Peace without justice is false and even dangerous. At the same time, justice does not solve all conflicts and bring peace. It might bring order, but not joy, well-being, and life. One must go beyond justice, and this is why Jesus gave us the new commandment of love (John 13). To live out this vision of beloved community, shalom, and the kingdom of God, we must strive nonviolently for justice and love in every area of our lives.

How do we participate in this vision in our daily life? Before I offer a few ways, allow me to explain about the trifold paradigm of violence, a concept introduced by sociologist Johan Galtung, who is known as the father of peace studies. Galtung differentiates between three types of violence: direct violence, structural violence, and cultural violence. He explains that the cause of direct violence is often linked to structural violence and justified by cultural violence. Like the tip of an iceberg, direct violence is visible, but structural violence and cultural violence are hidden underneath direct violence, and so they are hard to identify. I will explain more about these types of violence in the sections that follow.

The trifold paradigm of violence helps us understand that Christian pacifism and nonviolence have to be lived out holistically. Not only must we know how to respond in the face of direct violence, but we must also know how to act against structural violence and cultural violence. While acknowledging that there are many ways of participating in the vision of beloved community in our daily lives, I will conclude this chapter by proposing two specific ways of doing so: (a) through confronting violent structures and transforming them into nonviolent ones, and (b) by challenging cultural violence and creating a culture of peace.

FROM VIOLENT TO NONVIOLENT STRUCTURES

Social structure is a social arrangement of human relationships on various levels, from macro to micro scale, where institutions, social norms, and value systems are interconnected. The national economy, social classes, educational systems, family, religions, legal systems, and political systems are all part of a social structure. Social structures influence and shape people's identities, interests, and interactions, and they can either limit or advance people's actions and decisions. Since we all depend on our social structures, they are pivotal for our safety and well-being, but unfortunately, some social structures cause violence. We call these structures violent structures, or systems, and the violence that these structures (or systems) cause we call structural violence.

Structural violence refers to the physical, psychological, and spiritual harm that certain groups of people experience as a result of the unequal distribution of power and privilege. . . .

Structural violence degrades, dehumanizes, damages, and kills people by limiting or preventing their access to the necessities of life or for its flourishing."[4] Some examples of structural violence are institutionalized racism, sexism, ageism, and ethnocentrism. While identifying and punishing a perpetrator of direct violence is relatively easy, it is difficult to pinpoint who is responsible for the damage caused by structural violence, even though both types of violence are lethal. For example, when someone kills another person with a gun, that is direct violence. When a certain neighborhood is at a high risk of gun violence because of a lack of social services and funding for education, that is structural violence. When a woman is verbally and physically abused in a workplace, that is direct violence, but when women are paid less and denied opportunities to be promoted even though they have worked as much as or more than their male colleagues, that is structural violence.

We live in a democratic society where we emphasize equality, liberty, and justice, yet we still have numerous social structures that perpetrate violence. While contemporary social structures do not necessarily cause overt and direct violence, as did the ones that Gandhi and King confronted, they are similarly detrimental. In creating the beloved community, we need to unmask, reveal, and challenge the violent structures that exist among us. Also, since structural violence is not as visible as direct violence, we need to discern whether we are somehow complicit, including simply consenting to a certain structural violence. For instance, by buying products from companies that use child labor, we are being complicit to that structural violence, even though we are not directly involved in the decision-making of the companies. When we are silent at our workplace when a female colleague is being treated unjustly, we are also partaking in structural violence.

After discerning and challenging a specific source of structural violence, the next step is to transform the violent structure into a **nonviolent structure** by creating structures and systems that protect the weak, treat people with respect, offer equal distribution of power and privilege, and strive for the flourishing of each person and community. This is what social movements like the women's rights movement, the environmental movement, the animal rights movement, the Black Lives Matter movement, the Chicano movement, the civil rights movement, the fair trade movement, the LGBT rights movement, the Indigenous peoples movement, the labor movements, the Me Too movement, and Occupy Wall Street have been participants in. As we participate in God's kingdom, when we see injustice done through structural violence, especially to marginalized people and communities, it is our responsibility to be in solidarity with the suffering people, to challenge violent structures, and to transform them into nonviolent ones that support and enrich the lives of everyone.

CREATING A CULTURE OF PEACE

Johan Galtung asserts that to dismantle structural violence, one must also be involved in challenging **cultural violence**, because cultural violence justifies and even legitimizes direct and structural violence.[5] The myth of redemptive violence is one example of cultural violence. The belief that Latinos are lazy, that all Muslims are terrorists, or that men are superior to women are some other examples of cultural violence. Because of these beliefs, some companies pay higher salaries to men than women, and some cities restrict Muslim women from wearing hijabs and niqabs.

In challenging cultural violence, it is important to identify and name distorted beliefs that are linked to cultural violence.

Some other distorted beliefs that are widely accepted in our society are the belief in scarcity and the belief that humans are the center of the world. The belief in scarcity, although it is not the only cause of inequality, is used to justify the unequal distribution of resources and privilege. However, God's creation story stands against this belief. Because we believe in the God of abundance who created the world, we can enjoy life in abundance. Yet as Gandhi said, we have enough resources for everyone's needs, but not for everyone's greed.

The belief that humans are the most important beings on the planet and that they are the center of the world has led people to exploit nature, pollute the environment, and create factory farming where animals are treated in a cruel way just for human convenience and consumption. Rather than find ways to coexist with nature and respect the land, air, plants, and animals, we try to dominate them for our own convenience. Consequently, we have caused vast amounts of violence and destruction to all living beings in this world, including ourselves. We have polluted the ocean with plastic, we incessantly consume and create trash, and we poison our environment. We need to renounce this belief and recognize that we are merely stewards of God's beautiful creation and have the obligation to take care of and look after nature.

In identifying cultural violence, we need at least two specific practices: (a) we need to allow God's truth to speak to us through the Bible and to reflect critically together as a body of Christ to determine whether some of our beliefs are causing cultural violence; and (b) it is vital to listen attentively to the voices of marginalized people. When we are in the dominant group and when life is structured around people who are similar to us, we do not see how our social structure and cultural beliefs are causing harm to marginalized groups. For this reason, we need to hear the voices of minorities and to try to see what kinds of oppression and violence they are experiencing. Living in North America, where Christianity historically has been the dominant religion, we need to hear what kind of injustices and inequality people from other religions are experiencing. We live in a society where patriarchy still exists. That reality has ramifications, especially for those of us who are male and who desire justice. We continually need to hear what women are experiencing and to work together to challenge cultural violence and create a **culture of peace**, where everyone is welcomed, loved, and treated justly.

Challenging structural and cultural violence and creating nonviolent structures and a culture of peace are holistic approaches to reducing various types of violence that are pervasive in our lives. Let's briefly examine one example, domestic violence, a type of violence that is widespread in society. According to research done by the National Center for Injury Prevention and Control of the Centers for Disease Control and Prevention, one in four women and one in nine men have experienced severe violence by an intimate partner in the United States. Also, an average of twenty people experience physical violence from their intimate partner every minute, which equates to more than ten million victims yearly.[6] To prevent and reduce violence between intimate partners, the CDC advises six strategies: (a) teach safe and healthy relationship skills, (b) engage influential adults and peers, (c) disrupt the developmental pathways toward partner violence, (d) create protective environments, (e) strengthen economic supports for families, and (f) support survivors to increase safety and lessen harms.[7]

Although this is not an exhaustive list, one can note that these strategies not only emphasize the need for direct action against domestic violence but also challenge and transform structural and cultural violence and create nonviolent structures and cultures of peace. The CDC understands that a holistic approach is needed to reduce domestic violence. Moreover, in making these changes, we need to recognize that it is an endeavor done not individually, but communally. After providing these six strategies, the CDC encourages individuals and groups to engage in these strategies with several organizations, such as public health agencies, social services, health services, business groups, local, regional, and national justice departments, housing services, community organizations, media, and domestic violence coalitions. Clearly, a holistic approach is needed to reduce violence and build peace, and this work should be done collaboratively with various communities and organizations. And in these tasks, it is vital for churches to be actively engaged.

I would like to conclude by pondering the topic of power. Commonly, power is viewed negatively. This is mostly because we have heard and seen the ways that people in power have abused their power. Some Christians believe that we should discard power and try to become powerless. They advocate for this position by emphasizing that Jesus became powerless when he was taken to the cross. Nevertheless, the more I meditate on power, the more I have learned that we all have a certain amount of power. What Jesus has taught is not powerlessness, but rather how to use power in the right way, to resist evil nonviolently.

The Romans had multiple methods of executing criminals, but reserved crucifixion, which required a huge amount of effort and time to implement, for those whose actions threatened the Roman hold on power. If the Romans had simply hated Jesus or were forced to terminate him, they could have chosen an easier way to execute him. They crucified Jesus because they wanted to tell all the people who would witness or hear of his death to obey the authority of the Roman Empire. This means that the Romans saw Jesus as a dangerous figure who could subvert the empire. Jesus was an active resister who spoke against the injustices of the Jewish faith and of the Roman Empire of that time, but he continually practiced the love of enemy. As a consequence, he was crucified. Jesus accepted the sacrifice and the death that came as a result of nonviolent resistance. Jesus was not powerless; he showed much power that was connected to the love of enemy. Jesus' example reminds me of what Martin Luther King Jr. once said: "What is needed is a realization that power without love is reckless and abusive and that love without power is sentimental and anemic. Power at its best is love implementing the demands of justice."[8]

We need to ask how we are going to use our power when injustice occurs, when we are oppressed. Are we going to use violence to retaliate, or are we going to resist nonviolently? Both methods require power, but one method is done because of a lack of love, and one is full of love. Which one will you choose? The beloved community, shalom, and the kingdom of God will be achieved by people who love their neighbors *and* enemies powerfully, by people who show a powerful love that is based on justice, as Jesus, who is our Prince of Peace, has shown.

"For God did not give us a spirit of cowardice, but rather a spirit of power and of love and of self-discipline."
—2 Timothy 1:7

Glossary

beloved community: A term first used by philosopher Josiah Royce and popularized by Martin Luther King Jr. It envisions the transformation of discrimination to fairness, hatred to love, injustice to justice, and enmity to reconciliation. It seeks a new relationship between the oppressed and the oppressors and a new way of living where wealth and resources are fairly shared so that every person and community can flourish.

Christian pacifism: A way of life that embodies Jesus' teaching of the love of neighbors and love toward enemies. Not only does it oppose war, but it also stands against all forms of violence that exist in human life and relationships.

cultural violence: Any cultural aspect that encourages and justifies direct and structural violence. Cultural violence can be found in religion, ideology, media, education, art, science, and other cultural elements.

culture of peace: A way of living that rejects violence and finds nonviolent and creative ways to engage and possibly transform conflict. It seeks to welcome and treat everyone and everything respectfully, including animals and all of nature.

historic peace churches: The three main groups represented are the Mennonites, the Church of the Brethren, and the Religious Society of Friends (Quakers). The term historic peace churches emerged from a joint meeting in Kansas in 1935. From the beginning of their existence, these groups have been committed to peace.

just peacemaking: A paradigm that seeks to prevent conflicts from escalating to war and to diminish wars. It is a concept that combines pacifism's commitment to nonviolence and the realistic aspects of just war theory. As a result of several discussions, scholars and activists from various Christian traditions and different fields of study developed a list of ten practices for people, churches, and governments to apply.

just war theory: A view that permits violence under certain conditions but also attempts to restrict it by limiting the valid causes for participating in a war and by restricting certain actions during a war.

myth of redemptive violence: A belief that even though violence is a terrible thing, it is a necessary evil to bring peace, to fight against a greater evil, and to save us from danger.

nonviolence: Mahatma Gandhi was the first person to clearly articulate and popularize this term. It means an active resistance to bring about social and political change without using violence. It is usually used in the context of a campaign for social change and revolution.

nonviolent structure: A social structure that protects the weak, treats people with respect, offers equal distribution of power and privilege, and strives for the well-being of all people.

shalom: The central vision of the Bible that is depicted in the Old Testament where all creation is in community with one another and living in harmony. Shalom becomes a reality when there is peace in the relationships between God and human beings, humans with others, humans with nature and environment, and humans with their inner selves.

structural violence: A certain type of violence that causes physical, psychological, and/or spiritual harm to particular people because of the unequal distribution of wealth, resources, power, and privileges.

Discussion and Reflection Questions

INTRODUCTION

1. Who are your enemies and how do you know? How have you been treating them?
2. What advice and comments have you heard about how to treat enemies?

CHAPTER 1

1. Did your perspective of Jesus change after reading this chapter? If yes, how? If no, why not?
2. What other interpretations of Matthew 5:38-41 have you heard? Are those interpretations helpful in engaging with your enemies? Why or why not?
3. What are some new ways of applying the teaching of Matthew 5:38-41 in your own culture and community?

CHAPTER 2

1. What was your reaction after reading Dirk Willems's story? Do you see his action as courageous or foolish? Why?

2. What are some of your fears? Where do you think those fears come from? In the midst of fear, what specific actions can you take to trust more in God?

3. Think of a situation where you had to confront your enemies or someone who treated you wrongly. Imagine that situation and apply the two hands of nonviolence. What would you say and do differently this time?

CHAPTER 3

1. What are your thoughts on just war theory? What are some aspects with which you agree or disagree?

2. How do you draw a line between coercive force and lethal violence? What are some distinctions? Why is drawing this line tricky?

3. What are your thoughts on the myth of redemptive violence? Do you think this way of thinking is widespread, as the author states?

4. Where else can you identify the myth of redemptive violence in your everyday life?

CHAPTER 4

1. How do people in contemporary society commonly view pacifists? Do you agree with that view? Why or why not?

2. Research your church denomination and find out what your church's position is on war and peace. What are the arguments for supporting a certain stance?

3. What other responses to war can Christian pacifists have?

4. What practices among the ten practices of just peacemaking can your small group or church community enact?

CHAPTER 5

1. What do you think about the research presented by Erica Chenoweth and Maria Stephan? Do you find it convincing? Why or why not?

2. What concerns or comments do you have for nonviolent campaigns?

3. Is there a particular nonviolent campaign that your church would like to start or be involved in? If yes, share what it is and how you might plan to get involved.

CHAPTER 6

1. How can you and your community work on creating beloved community?

2. What are some types of structural violence you can identify in your community and neighborhood? What can you do concretely to change violent structures?

3. What types of cultural violence can you identify? What can your church do to create a culture of peace?

4. What is your general understanding of power? How does the understanding of power introduced in this chapter help you?

Shared Convictions

Mennonite World Conference, a global community of Christian churches that facilitates community between Anabaptist-related churches, offers these shared convictions that characterize Anabaptist faith. For more on Anabaptism, go to ThirdWay.com.

By the grace of God, we seek to live and proclaim the good news of reconciliation in Jesus Christ. As part of the one body of Christ at all times and places, we hold the following to be central to our belief and practice:

1. God is known to us as Father, Son and Holy Spirit, the Creator who seeks to restore fallen humanity by calling a people to be faithful in fellowship, worship, service and witness.

2. Jesus is the Son of God. Through his life and teachings, his cross and resurrection, he showed us how to be faithful disciples, redeemed the world, and offers eternal life.

3. As a church, we are a community of those whom God's Spirit calls to turn from sin, acknowledge Jesus Christ as Lord, receive baptism upon confession of faith, and follow Christ in life.

4. As a faith community, we accept the Bible as our authority for faith and life, interpreting it together under Holy Spirit guidance, in the light of Jesus Christ to discern God's will for our obedience.

5. The Spirit of Jesus empowers us to trust God in all areas of life so we become peacemakers who renounce violence, love our enemies, seek justice, and share our possessions with those in need.

6. We gather regularly to worship, to celebrate the Lord's Supper, and to hear the Word of God in a spirit of mutual accountability.

7. As a world-wide community of faith and life we transcend boundaries of nationality, race, class, gender and language. We seek to live in the world without conforming to the powers of evil, witnessing to God's grace by serving others, caring for creation, and inviting all people to know Jesus Christ as Saviour and Lord.

In these convictions we draw inspiration from Anabaptist forebears of the 16th century, who modelled radical discipleship to Jesus Christ. We seek to walk in his name by the power of the Holy Spirit, as we confidently await Christ's return and the final fulfillment of God's kingdom

Adopted by Mennonite World Conference General Council, March 15, 2006

Acknowledgments

I wish to thank Jinah Im, Justin Lee, Susan Riggs, Trent Voth, and Young Seok Yoo for carefully reading through the early draft of my writing and offering helpful comments and advice. I am also grateful for Dayna Olson-Getty and her team of editors at Herald Press for all their hard work in editing and enhancing the manuscript.

I am indebted to Valerie Weaver-Zercher, who approached me and gave me the wonderful opportunity to write this book. Without her invitation, this book would not exist.

Notes

Chapter 1

1 Gerard A. Vanderhaar, *Enemies and How to Love Them* (Mystic, CT: Twenty-Third Publications, 1985), 67.

2 Walter Wink, *Engaging the Powers*, 25th anniv. ed. (Minneapolis: Augsburg Fortress, 2017), 189.

Chapter 2

1 John S. Oyer and Robert S. Kreider, *Mirror of the Martyrs: Stories of Courage, Inspiring Retold, of 16th Century Anabaptists Who Gave Their Lives for Their Faith* (Intercourse, PA: Good Books, 2002), 36–37.

2 Arash Javanbakht and Linda Saab, "The Science of Fright: Why We Love to Be Scared," The Conversation, October 26, 2017, https://theconversation.com/the-science-of-fright-why-we-love-to-be-scared-85885?xid=PS_smithsonian.

3 John Roth, *Choosing against War: A Christian View* (Intercourse, PA: Good Books, 2002), 103.

4 Ibid, 108.

5 See John Howard Yoder, *The Politics of Jesus: Vicit Agnus Noster*, 2nd ed. (Grand Rapids, MI: Eerdmans, 1994), 228–47.

6 See John Howard Yoder, *Nevertheless: The Varieties and Short-comings of Religious Pacifism*, rev. ed. (Scottdale, PA: Herald Press, 2001), 11–14.

7 I am aware of the sexual abuse and other abuses of power that John Howard Yoder committed and of how, therefore, he failed to live as a faithful disciple. Yet I still think some of his insights are useful, and so I cautiously refer to a few of his ideas.

8 David Augsburger, *Dissident Discipleship: A Spirituality of Self-Surrender, Love of God, and Love of Neighbor* (Grand Rapids, MI: Brazos Press, 2006), 142–43.

9 *Oxford English Dictionary Online*, s.v. "enemy," accessed August 7, 2019, https://www-oed-com.myaccess.library.utoronto.ca/view/Entry/62058?rskey=jFPIzv&result=1.

Chapter 3

1 Walter Wink, "The Myth of Redemptive Violence," *The Bible in TransMission*, Spring 1999, 7.

2 United States Conference of Catholic Bishops, "The Harvest of Justice Is Sown in Peace," USCCB, accessed August 7, 2019, http://www.usccb.org/beliefs-and-teachings/what-we-believe/catholic-social-teaching/the-harvest-of-justice-is-sown-in-peace.cfm.

3 John Dear, *Put Down Your Sword: Answering the Gospel Call to Creative Nonviolence* (Grand Rapids, MI: Eerdmans, 2008), 4.

Chapter 4

1 Brian Doyle, *Saints Passionate and Peculiar: Brief Exuberant Essays for Teens* (Winona, MN: Saint Mary's Press, 2002), 27–28.

2 Henry A. Hubert and John H. Redekop, "Christians and War," Canadian Conference of Mennonite Brethren Churches, accessed August 7, 2019, https://www.mennonitebrethren.ca/nflt-resources/christians-and-war/.

3 General Board of the General Conference Mennonite Church and the Mennonite Church General Board, *Confession of Faith in a Mennonite Perspective* (Harrisonburg, VA: Herald Press, 1995), available at http://mennoniteusa.org/confession-of-faith/.

4 See Glen Stassen, ed., *Just Peacemaking: The New Paradigm for the Ethics of Peace and War* (Cleveland: Pilgrim Press, 2008).

5 Glen Stassen and David Gushee, *Kingdom Ethics: Following Jesus in Contemporary Context* (Downers Grove, IL: InterVarsity Press, 2003), 174.

Chapter 5

1 Erica Chenoweth, "The Success of Nonviolent Civil Resistance," filmed September 2013 in Boulder, CO, TED video, 12:33, https://www.youtube.com/watch?v=YJSehRlU34w.

2 Ibid.

3 King offered these steps in his *Letter from Birmingham Jail*, and the King Center has adapted and expanded them. See "The King Philosophy," The King Center, accessed August 7, 2019, https://thekingcenter.org/king-philosophy/.

4 See Gene Sharp, "198 Methods of Nonviolent Action," Albert Einstein Institution, accessed March 9, 2020, https://www.aeinstein.org/nonviolentaction/198-methods-of-nonviolent-action/.

5 See Gene Sharp, *The Dynamics of Nonviolent Action*, vol. 3 of *The Politics of Nonviolent Action* (Boston: Porter Sargent, 1973), 657–58.

6 Gene Sharp, *Waging Nonviolent Struggle: 20th Century Practice and 21st Century Potential* (Boston: Porter Sargent, 2005), 384, 410–12.

Chapter 6

1 Martin Luther King Jr., "I Have a Dream" (address, March on Washington for Jobs and Freedom, Washington, DC, August 28, 1963),
text available at https://kinginstitute.stanford.edu/king-papers/documents/i-have-dream-address-delivered-march-washington-jobs-and-freedom.

2 Martin Luther King Jr., "Palm Sunday Sermon on Mohandas K. Gandhi" (sermon, Dexter Avenue Baptist Church, Montgomery, AL, March 22, 1959), text available at https://kinginstitute.stanford.edu/king-papers/documents/palm-sunday-sermon-mohandas-k-gandhi-delivered-dexter-avenue-baptist-church.

3 Walter Brueggemann, *Peace*, Understanding Biblical Themes (St. Louis: Chalice Press, 2001), 13–14.

4 Cynthia Moe-Lobeda, *Resisting Structural Evil: Love as Ecological-Economic Vocation* (Minneapolis: Fortress Press, 2013), 72.

5 Johan Galtung, "Violence, Peace, and Peace Research," *Journal of Peace Research* 6, no. 3 (1969): 291.

6 Michele C. Black et al., *The National Intimate Partner and Sexual Violence Survey (NISVS): 2010 Summary Report* (Atlanta: National Center for Injury Prevention and Control, Centers for Disease Control and Prevention, 2011).

7 Phyllis Holditch Niolon et al., *Preventing Intimate Partner Violence across the Lifespan: A Technical Package of Programs, Policies, and Practices* (Atlanta: National Center for Injury Prevention and Control, Centers for Disease Control and Prevention, 2017).

8 Martin Luther King Jr., "Where Do We Go from Here: Chaos or Community?," in *A Testament of Hope: The Essential Writings and Speeches of Martin Luther King Jr.*, ed. James M. Washington (San Francisco: Harper San Francisco, 1991), 578.

The Author

Hyung Jin Kim Sun, also known as Pablo, is a Korean-Paraguayan Mennonite and a PhD candidate in theological ethics at Emmanuel College in the Toronto School of Theology. He works as a teaching, research, and program assistant at the Forum for Intercultural Leadership and Learning, a reference group of the Canadian Council of Churches. After completing his undergraduate studies in Asunción, Paraguay, Kim Sun earned an MA and MDiv at Fuller Theological Seminary, where he met and married his wif, Jinah. He also holds a ThM from Boston College. Kim Sun became a Mennonite because of his strong conviction in the gospel of peace. He serves as an assistant pastor at Toronto Mennonite New Life Church.

SMALL BOOKS · **THE** · **JESUS** · **WAY** · of **RADICAL FAITH**

HERALD PRESS

www.HeraldPress.com. 1-800-245-7894